MESSENGERS

Portraits of
African American
Ministers, Evangelists,
Gospel Singers, and
Other Messengers
of the Word

MESSENGERS

David Ritz

Photographs by Nicola Goode

DOUBLEDAY
New York London Toronto Sydney Auckland

PUBLISHED BY DOUBLEDAY
a division of Random House, Inc.

DOUBLEDAY and the portrayal of an anchor with a dolphin
are registered trademarks of Random House, Inc.

Book design by Elizabeth Rendfleisch

Library of Congress Cataloging-in-Publication Data
Ritz, David.
Messengers : portraits of African American ministers, evangelists, gospel singers, and other
messengers of the Word / David Ritz; photographer, Nicola Goode.—1st ed.
p. cm.
1. African Americans—Religion. 2. African American clergy—Biography. 3. African American
evangelists—Biography. 4. African American gospel singers—Biography. 5. African Americans—
Biography. I. Title.
BR563.N4R58 2005
277.3'082'092396073—dc22
[B]
2005049654

ISBN 0-385-51395-X

PRINTED IN JAPAN

April 2006
First Edition

1   3   5   7   9   10   8   6   4   2

FOR MY SISTER ELIZABETH,

WHOSE LOVING HEART LED THE WAY

CONTENTS

Contents

Contents

Contents

Contents

Warm gratitude to Janet Hill, Steve Rubin, Tracy Jacobs, Reisig and Taylor Photography, Dennis Franklin, Skip Smith, John Tayloe, Sheila Goode, Dylan McFarland, Fritz Goode, Sean McFarland, Dejon Mayes, Kevin King, Howard Hewett, Glenn Kiser, Karl Kakadelis, Harry Weinger, Leo Sacks, Herb Powell, Pascal Pinck, Milton Ritz, Roberta Ritz, Alison Ritz, Jessica Ritz, Esther Ritz, Charlotte Pearl, Jim Jack, Henry Alonso Myers, and Alan Eisenstock.

And to all the Messengers, thank you for your time and inspiration.

INTRODUCTION

In the course of writing this book I became a Christian. In fact, one of the ministers included in this collection of testimonies—Dr. Mable John—presided at my baptism. I say this to explain that the energy driving this project is both personal and passionate.

It took me some six decades to finally embrace Jesus. For years I secretly called His name in midnight prayers when I was overwhelmed by my fear of the dark, incurable disease, and the terrifying notion of death itself. I fantasized about being a believer but never knew how to get there. As a Jew, I cherished then as I cherish now the cultural and intellectual riches of my heritage. My religious indoctrinations, though—my bar mitzvah and confirmation—were more social than sacred. I never felt the spirit of God. Strangely enough, the first time I felt that spirit was in a ballpark used to house a concert. It happened in the mid-fifties in Dallas, Texas, when I was fourteen. As a member of a family of transplanted New Yorkers, I was an outsider in alien territory. As a kid in love with jazz, I missed the music I had heard in Manhattan—Miles Davis, Thelonious Monk, Billie Holiday. But on Dallas radio stations I heard other music that excited me as much: rhythm and blues and gospel. Except for the words, they sounded similar. The voices thrilled me. The raw power and sincerity of the voices warmed my heart and gave me courage to muddle through a mess of teenage fears.

On that summer night in the ballpark, I went to see Mahalia Jackson. I watched her fans file in—women in bright dresses and big hats, men in sharp suits. Even though the city was segregated, there was no separate seating. Except for myself and a handful of others, the crowd was black. Mahalia appeared in white, her dress a mass of cascading white ruffles and white lace, the high white hat atop her beehive hairdo a regal crown. Standing in the center of the field, she spoke authoritatively. "Been singing all over the world," she said. "Been singing in fancy concert halls where even kings and queens have come to hear what all the shouting's about. I like that, but I like this more. This is singing to the folk who knew me back when." But before she could sing, a sudden electric buzz broke the spell and killed the sound. Mahalia simply stood there, hands on her ample hips. "They had singin' before electricity," she shouted out. "And they gonna have singin' after all the electricity in the world blows itself up. And we gonna have us some singin' tonight." And with that she pushed the microphone aside and sang. Sang loud enough to be heard all over the world. Sang with a joy that had me leaping to my feet. Sang with an energy that connected me to something so deep, so true, so genuine, so extravagant, so strong, so stimulating, so absolutely convincing that I believed every word. I believed her when she sang about the love of Jesus, the truth of Jesus, the power of Jesus to heal and transform lives. I wanted my life transformed. Without telling anyone, without admitting it to the world, that night I secretly accepted Jesus into my heart.

It took me a lifetime to return to that simple acceptance. In the meantime, I grew up a secularist. I went to good colleges and married a wonderful woman with whom I had two wonderful daughters. I followed the voices that had called to me as a child. I became a ghostwriter so I could absorb those voices and project them onto the page. I never met Mahalia, but I met Ray Charles and then I met Marvin Gaye, who spoke to me of the same Jesus Mahalia had sung about. Marvin was confused and conflicted, but he was my idol and his love for Jesus was contagious. When Marvin was clear, centered, and calm, he exuded a sweetness and easygoing grace that felt divine. I saw Jesus in Marvin. I heard Jesus in Marvin's voice. I was an eager student and Marvin an eager teacher when it came to the lessons of the Lord. As his friend and biographer, I watched Marvin struggle with those lessons before he finally fell victim to his fears.

It took me another two decades to face my own fears. It took admitting that those fears had fueled a network of addictions. It took—and still takes—the loving wisdom of twelve-step programs to allow me, a day at a time, to break free of those addictions. It took examining the history of those programs to understand that their inspiration was the transformational power of the same Jesus whom Marvin and Mahalia had praised in song. And it took going back to that summer night in the ballpark when I accepted my need to be comforted by a spirit beyond my comprehension.

Today I love calling that spirit Jesus. His name resonates in every fiber of my being. His name sings of compassion, forgiveness, and inexhaustible love. His name holds the magic of all the music of the spheres. That music calls to me when He says, "Come to Me, all you who are weary and burdened, and I will give you rest. Take my yoke upon you and learn from me, for I am gentle and humble in heart, and you will find rest for your souls. For my yoke is easy and my burden is light." When He beckons me to come to Him as a child, I put down the burdens of my overworked adult brain and, like a child, receive His reassuring presence.

Seeking that presence is the main motive of this book. Because I first felt His presence in the voices of African

Americans, those were the voices I sought when I committed to strengthening my faith. I wanted the music and the magic that those voices contain. I wanted to hear about Jesus in intimate conversations. I wanted to feel Jesus through words that would melt my intellectual resistance—my overthinking and overanalysis—and directly address my heart. To find the messengers who spoke those words meant following the prompts of my heart. Those prompts directed me to diversity: women and men; young, old, and middle-aged; ministers and musicians; singers and teachers; preachers known throughout the world and preachers known only in their neighborhoods. My only requirement was that their message reflect the grace and glory of God.

My journey was blessed from the get-go, first by my wonderful editor, Janet Hill, whose faith made this project possible, and then by my collaborator, the gifted photographer Nicola Goode, whose glowing portraits caught each messenger's unique inner light. A further blessing came in a frightening form. Shortly after my baptism, I was diagnosed with kidney cancer. Suddenly my strongest childhood fears were knocking at the door. At first, fear enveloped me. Fear lingered, expanded, threatened. I wondered whether I could handle it, whether my faith would prove a sham and I would somehow lose it. I turned to the voices—singing voices and talking voices, teaching voices and preaching voices— and heard the one voice that invited me to believe, accept, and trust. That voice saw me through a successful operation. That voice sustained me through a challenging recovery. That voice, in various expressions, is what I hope you hear as you read this book. That voice—joyful, strong, and clear—is the good news gospel of Jesus, whose message defeats death and declares victory, now and forever, in the precious name of love.

—David Ritz

"... he who receives and welcomes and takes into his heart any messenger of Mine receives Me."

—John 13:20 (Amplified Bible)

SATURATE THE HOUSE WITH PRAISE

DR. MABLE JOHN

It happened onstage in Birmingham, Alabama. I was a Raelette, a background vocalist for my friend Ray Charles. We were singing "What'd I Say." Near the end of the song, Ray sings, "Baby, let's go home," and the

Raelettes answer, "Yes, let's go home." While singing those words I was suddenly jolted by a voice saying, *"Go home, Mable. I have something for you to do."* The voice was clear as day. I looked around, but no one was there. I realized I had heard the voice of God.

That voice led me home to God. That voice also led me to leave the field of popular music and study God's Word. I studied for a solid decade. Learned Greek to read the original-language Bible, earned a Ph.D. from UCLA in counseling, graduated from an accredited school of ministry.

Then the Lord spoke again: *"I'm not sending you to Beverly Hills to minister to the rich. I'm sending you to the streets to feed the poor."* So I set up a ministry in a big house in South Central Los

Angeles, where we prayed every morning at 5 A.M. and studied the Word every day at noon. Once a week we fed the hungry. "When's the next feeding?" asked a man who'd arrived a day late. "Next Tuesday," I said. "Next Tuesday," he said, "I may be dead." His statement grieved my spirit until my ministry expanded to more frequent feedings. We witnessed miracles. Four crack houses operating down the street suddenly shut down. Drug dealers vanished. Worshippers appeared. We stopped people from picking food out of dumpsters and invited them to our table. We clothed hundreds of families. But when the house was burglarized, I knew I had to move. And, sure enough, the voice of God returned, repeating the words I had heard that night onstage: "*Go home, Mable.*"

So my home became my church. My home became the physical center of my faith. My home and my heart and the heart of God dwelled in the same place. Jesus took up residence in my home. Volunteers arrived. Over Thanksgiving and Christmas, blessings arrived. We fed thousands. We clothed thousands. On Sunday mornings, we sang songs and I spoke of my love for the Lord. That love—that gratitude and appreciation of His grace—deepens with every year.

I'm grateful for the experience of my past. When I started out, I wanted everything my way. I was in a hurry. I was interested in accomplishment and knew little about patience. As a young woman in Detroit, I was minister of music for the state of Michigan. Outside of music, I worked as a registered nurse. Then Berry Gordy, founder of Motown, signed me as the first female solo artist on his new label. Later, along with Otis Redding and Isaac Hayes, I made records for the Stax label, a pioneer in the field of sixties soul music. I wrote hit songs. But as I moved through life, as I discovered my need for God and admitted my helplessness to operate without him, my attitude changed. My patience deepened. I learned to talk to the Father and take my problems to prayer. I learned that prayer strengthens me. I learned that God has the answers; that prayer lets Him feed those answers to my heart; that when you serve a living God, faith is your constant friend; that no challenge is too big for the Lord; no burden too great, no grief too deep.

Not long ago, my mother, sister, and two of my sons passed away, all within ten months. A friend asked how I managed. "I saturate the house with praise," I said. "I stay strong before God so I can do what I have to do." I promised these loved ones that I would walk them through every valley and up every mountain until they were delivered into the arms of Jesus. Even on the worst days, I woke up every morning praising God for the privilege of serving someone, praising God my sustainer, God my deliverer.

I call my ministry Joy in Jesus because, regardless of the circumstances, serving God guarantees joy. At seventy-four, my energy is good, my back straight, and my mission—to make Jesus real to those who don't know Him—a source of undying comfort and selfless love.

ENNOBLING, ENABLING, EMPOWERING

REVEREND PROFESSOR PETER J. GOMES

I was eight
years old when
we had a little
ceremony at
our Sunday
school as we
moved from
primary to
intermediate
classes. The
pastor gave
each child
Scripture he
called our "life
verse." Mine
was Romans

12:1 and 2. "I beseech you, therefore, brethren, by the mercies of God that you present your bodies a living sacrifice, wholly acceptable under God, which is your reasonable service. Do not be conformed to this world but be transformed by the renewing of your mind." The minister inscribed those words in my Bible and instructed me to memorize them. I have never forgotten them. In fact, I can still recite all of Romans 12. The minister was right: This was the key to my life.

That verse made all the difference. I can't call it a road to Damascus phenomenon, but I can say it planted the seed within. It introduced me to the idea of transformation. Being a follower of Jesus means that we are transformed from what we were. Transformation is everything. The gospel we love is a gospel of transformation and nonconformity. The good news is that this world is not all there is. This is not the world to which we trim our sails. This is not the world from which we seek our identity. The miracle is in the spiritual metamorphosis. Looking back some fifty-eight years to that singular moment when I received those precious words, I see that was the start of a process that continues to this day. My life, my ministry, my career, my personality have all been one of nonconformity and transformation into the mind of Christ.

Here in Cambridge, where I have served as a minister and professor at Harvard for many years, I have preached to the brightest and best. I have also preached to the dullest and the least. Regardless of my constituency, the message remains the same: God is invested in us. We don't know why. I, for one, certainly don't deserve it. But God has employed us as agents of change in His kingdom. He has said to me, "Gomes, you have talent, and I'm going to make that talent work for Me. I'm going to make *you* work for Me." He says that to us all. All of us have talent. The trick is recognizing and then utilizing that talent in His service. That's our life work—expressing His energy through our own personalities. It might be in preaching or in conversation or in witnessing or in simply being faithful. It might be in matters great but most especially in matters small.

For many years I had doubts. Am I the right guy in the right place? Yet somehow my confidence grew. I have never been a modest man. But as an insecure man, I have watched that insecurity decline as my faith has risen. I am secure in making the case that, as believers in Jesus, we must be suspicious of other loyalties and labels, whether it's capitalism or communism, race or rank,

Ennobling, Enabling, Empowering

occupation or gender. I am both black and homosexual, but neither of those categories defines me. Christ defines me. I am His child. His servant. His follower. Other identities are more tangible. Others offer more short-term security. But my identity in Him is eternal. He is all I need.

I have no need to argue with other theologians whose views differ from my own. I was not brought to faith because I won an argument or lost an argument to someone smarter than me. I stand in a living relationship to Jesus Christ. He has invested in me and planned a design for me. I must make good on His investment; I must fulfill His design. My ministry and lifestyle have been attacked by people who subscribe to biblical inerrancy. I find inerrancy in total captivity to the terms of this world. The God I worship does not subscribe to those terms. But inerrancy is only a minor irritant along the way toward the knowledge of God. I avoid useless disputations.

My focus is on grace. Unmeritorious enablement. I preach grace by asking people to discover it for themselves in the very lives they've lived. Recognize what already has happened. Think of your worst day. Now realize you were delivered from that day. Realize that Jesus loves you. You may feel that you don't merit it. You may not even love Jesus. But that does not alter the fact that He loves you. And like it or not, that love is ennobling, enabling, empowering. That love makes it possible for you to get up and get on with your life. That love lets you say, "If Jesus loves me, maybe I can love myself."

Ennobling, Enabling, Empowering

A TEACHABLE HEART

SMOKIE NORFUL

Five short years ago, as a young man in my mid-twenties, I was teaching school, attending seminary, working as an assistant pastor, and writing songs in the basement. It was exhilarating but exhausting.

Today I tour the country as a gospel artist and my first two records have gone gold. I am astonished, humbled, and excited by the way God has changed my life.

I am astonished because I never thought it would turn out this way. I was born in Little Rock, but my dad's work as a Methodist minister had us moving all the time. It was in Tulsa where things got shaky for me. In my early teens I started to toy with trouble. Never got serious, but it could have. In fact, my best buddy wound up being the Most Wanted Man in Oklahoma. Dad and Mom must have sensed the need to move—God gave them that good sense—and so we went back to Arkansas. Pine Bluff had a tight sense of community and my dangerous days were behind me. My ambition kicked in. I saw I had a little gift for writing and wrote poems, at ten dollars a shot, for girls who wanted to express themselves to their boyfriends. I also knew God had given me musical talent and, at age fourteen, I flew off to Minneapolis to meet Prince, who was set to sign me as his answer to Tevin Campbell. Contracts were written but never signed because my dad, always my protector, made one simple point—there was no provision for my education. "What that says," he told Prince's people, "is that you don't care about my child." Two years later Capitol Records was set to sign me as a pop singer. Promises were made, then broken, and the signing never happened. But I still dreamed of fortune and fame.

Those dreams were pushed in a different direction when I first heard the great gospel artist Vanessa Bell Armstrong. She is the singer of all singers. I studied Vanessa Bell, emulated her, even tried incorporating her amazing technique into a style of my own. Rather than immediately pursue a singing career, though, I followed my father's lead and pursued an education and graduated from the University of Arkansas with a major in history. Taught history in junior high and high school, where my students taught me as much as I taught them. God gave me the beautiful gift of a teachable heart. God called me to Him. I answered that call by entering seminary and serving as assistant pastor for the Rock of Ages Baptist Church in the suburbs of Chicago. Meanwhile, my music ministry was calling night and day. I responded by writing songs, some of which were recorded by famous gospel groups. A quarter semester before receiving my master's of divinity, I received instead a recording contract as a gospel artist. Suddenly my life became my songs.

A hit song from my first album, "I Need You," was written before I had achieved even a hint of fame. I wrote it out of desperation. I wrote it as my own personal cry. I was twenty-seven, my wife twenty-six. She was diagnosed with cancer and told to have a hysterectomy. My father, the pillar of our family, required open-heart surgery. All the while, I kept singing the song, praying the line that said, "In You, Lord, I have victory." Victory came. The cancer diagnosis had been wrong. The hysterectomy wasn't needed. Our miracle child number one was born. Then miracle child number two was born. My dad survived the operation. Meanwhile, as I kept singing, as my songs found larger and larger audiences, I kept saying, "If you're desperate, borrow my cry. Share my faith. Say with me, 'In You, Lord, I have victory.' "

I like to think that my musical ministry is one of healing and hope. Jesus is the hope. Jesus is the healer. Jesus showed me that, as a young kid dreaming of becoming the next Prince, I was dreaming the wrong dream. To achieve the right dream meant getting the right education. It meant learning to write and teach and, above all, learning to maintain a teachable heart that illuminates the lessons of the Lord.

I HAVE HEARD THE VOICE OF GOD AND I WILL ANSWER HIM

BISHOP CAROLYN
TYLER GUIDRY

I'm humbled by being one of twenty presiding bishops who hold the highest position in the African Methodist Episcopal Church. From my home in Jamaica, I oversee ninety-four churches covering a vast

geographic area that includes the Dominican Republic, Haiti, Trinidad, Puerto Rico, all of South America, England, and Holland. I believe that's a great step for a church that in over two hundred years didn't have a single woman in this position. I'm amazed that I have reached this point because for years I boxed with God, hoping to keep myself out of this arena. Fortunately, God won the bout.

I was born in 1937 in Jackson, Mississippi, at a time when women didn't think in terms of preaching. You married, you had your children, you grew a good family. Starting at thirteen, I taught Sunday school and studied the Bible. In college I studied economics. In 1964, my husband and I moved to Los Angeles. We had five beautiful boys. I had a fine job as a loan officer for a major bank, where I helped convert the handwritten system to computers. My family joined the Second African Methodist Episcopal Church, where I worked in many ministries. All the while, the Lord was working on my heart. I felt God pushing me to preach. But I pushed back. "Don't call me, Lord," I said. "Call my husband. Let me be the wife of the preacher. Let me be the first lady who wears the big hat and sits in the front row."

Then one Sunday morning our pastor preached from Acts 1:8—"... you will receive power when the Holy Spirit has come upon you; and you shall be My witnesses..."—when I was suddenly transported from my place in the choir to a place of transformational insight. I saw myself preaching before thousands of people. Afterward, I found myself joining the altar call and telling my minister, "I have heard the voice of God and I will follow Him." I asked the Lord for an institution to prepare me and, proving He has a sense of humor, He sent me to a Bible school where, for all their great scholarship, the male teachers taught that women could not be called to preach. "Fine," I said to God, "I will sit here and I will learn, but I will never defend my calling." Why waste the energy? There was too much to learn.

By then it was the seventies, we had a beautiful daughter in addition to our five boys, and the challenge was acute: How do I come off my job at the bank to serve God full-time? How does my family survive without two salaries? I prayed. I fasted. I heard the Lord challenge my faith. "If you trust Me," he said, "you'll obey Me." That night at school a guest speaker quoted Matthew 28:19: "Go therefore and make disciples of all the nations . . ." I took the passage to heart, quit my job, and, as the first woman to be ordained an itinerant elder in our conference of A.M.E., accepted an assignment to lead a poor little church in Indio, California, at seventy-five dollars a week. The Lord blessed my decision. The Lord *was* my decision. Somehow the Lord provided. My husband found work, and the church grew. I preached the message that with God you are nothing less than first-class. The church had been told they were too poor to do ministry. I said otherwise. Using various resources, we successfully solicited money for a day-care center. We instituted outreach programs. We became first-class. Six years later I was transferred to a larger congregation where, under God's direction, we eventually bought the entire block around the church.

My husband died in 1988, which is when I moved back to Los

Angeles to pastor Walker Temple A.M.E. Church. At the end of 1995, the Lord spoke to me again and said, "Announce your candidacy for bishop." It took nearly ten years until I was elected. There were initial defeats, there was ego-crushing, but God saw me through. God prepared me for my new mission.

I married Don Guidry, a retired army officer, in 1996, and with my husband by my side I welcome the challenges ahead. My territory includes countries where schooling is insufficient and hungry children lack clothing. My mission is to provide physically as well as spiritually. I am always moved when I hear from young women who say that my life in ministry has been an inspiration. That motivates me even more to follow God and discern His will. When I hear His voice, I answer Him. I always have. I always will.

JESUS IS ABOUT CHANGE

PASTOR JESSE ANDRUS

It's taken me a while to learn to rest in the Lord, but I think I'm there. Don't get me wrong. I work hard. In fact, I work ten hours a day filling vending machines. Plus I have a window-washing business. But

the congregation I pastor—the Christian Praise Church in south-east Washington, D.C.—is the work that allows me to rest on a bed of spiritual faith. The Holy Ghost allows me to rest. Faith in the completed work of Jesus Christ allows me to rest.

I first got an inkling of this when I was working as a custodi-an in a maximum security correctional facility. My job was to clean up the mess hall. I was wiping windowsills when I came across a little card that quoted Matthew 11:28, saying, "Come to Me, all you who are weary and burdened, and I will give you rest."

That was the drawing verse, the verse that made me stop and rethink my life. It was a verse that got me thinking a different way. I always thought I needed to exert myself beyond myself to achieve. I had to strive harder, work longer hours, get better results than anyone else. Funny, but even after that verse led me deeper into the Word, even after I answered God's call to magnify His name, I still hadn't absorbed the lesson. In the beginning, I preached with a heavy hand. I was adamant. I was unyielding. Because I'm animated by nature, I banged home my points through insistence rather than understanding. As the pressures of pastoring got to me, I focused on force rather than compassion. My yoke wasn't easy and my burden wasn't light. Well, when the membership started dwindling and a few elders voiced concern, I had to look at myself. Was I condemning rather than loving? Was I coming on too strong? Was I expressing the Word of God through the Holy Spirit or my own ego?

We love and worship Jesus because Jesus is about change. He

changes us. I prayed for that change and, glory to God, that change came about. The change came out of the Lord's divinity and my humanity. I had to admit I was messing up. I had to be honest and frank about messing up with people in my church and people in my life. I had to expose my frailty. It was either that or become defensive and even more arrogant. But building myself up would mean tearing God down. I needed to do the opposite: I needed to build up God. I needed to get up and let Him work on me. I needed to change.

In part, change came by enrolling in a beautiful study, the Grace Ministries in Manassas, Virginia. A formal course in grace gave me the insight that the contrast is between force and yielding. Force is law. Force is effort. Force is striving. But grace is yielding.

Grace is allowing. Grace is embracing the gift of a love that comes free with faith. We don't earn it, don't achieve it. We simply and gratefully receive it. And once we receive it, love is in action.

The activation of love is linked to resting in the Lord. He's already done it. We just have to live it. The more we depend on Him, the less we worry about the world. The world will do whatever it does. I can't change the world. I can't even change anyone's heart. Only God can. I see stress as something we impose upon ourselves; stress is when we let the world get to us. But if we let Him, if we trust Him, if we believe His Word, God relieves that stress. The change is that I no longer worry. With all my responsibilities as a family man, a churchman, and a working man, I've learned to stay out of the results because the results belong to God. I don't get anxiety attacks. I don't wake up in a panic. I sleep like a baby. I rest knowing that I'm a vessel for His use. My hands are His hands. My eyes are His eyes. He is in me. His work is my work. And His yoke is easy, His burden is light.

WALKING EPISTLES

DR. ARLENE CHURN

I've been preaching since the age of four—since, in fact, the age of cognizance. This is my fifty-ninth year in ministry, and I've seen enormous changes— some progress and some retrogression. Because I have

more years behind me than in front of me, I have some historical perspective about the divide between those who accept women preachers and those who don't. Surprisingly, even in this modern era of supposed enlightenment, many young male ministers still struggle with emotional issues surrounding women. Perhaps more than ever, there are those who display disdain at the thought of accepting us as peers. For seventeen years I was pastor at a large church in Camden, New Jersey, where, from time to time, the question arose of a woman's right to preach. I was—and remain—unyielding in my conviction that God has sanctioned exalted positions for both genders in His great ministry. Look at Moses's sister Miriam and her astounding prophetic power. Look at Deborah, a queen and a judge. Look at the New Testament and see how the

Word confirms the equality of women in the sight of God. Paul is said to have established a sexual hierarchy, but if you follow Paul throughout his teachings, you must conclude that he saw women as fellow laborers in the service of the Lord. He urged wives to obey their husbands, but he also urged husbands to love their wives.

After I spent many years overseeing a large church, my obedience took me in another direction. I expanded my education and earned certification as a grief counselor. I've written extensively on the subject. Some call me a life coach. In this new phase of my walk with Christ, my privilege is to work with people traumatized by loss. Dealing with death has become my domain. I offer comfort whose source is God Himself. We worship a God who relieves us of pain—whether physical or emotional—if only we seek Him. For those who seek help from me, my first job is to do more than listen; my job is to *hear.* We listen with our ears; we hear with our hearts. Hearing is healing. For a person racked with pain, the mere fact of being heard is a blessing.

The emotions that go with grief can incapacitate the strongest soul. Rather than pass through the necessary stages of mourning, mourners get stuck. Some get stuck on denial. Many get stuck on anger. They cook angry, they work angry, they drive angry, they even sleep angry. Some get stuck on guilt—*why my sister and not me?* Some get stuck on shame—*how could my son have overdosed on drugs?* Some get stuck on a false picture of God—*how could He allow a baby to die?* My job is to pry loose those emotions and get the mourner to articulate, ventilate, and vocalize. My job is also to offer hope in the promise of a new life. That's why I say the end is the beginning. Hope, like love, is a commodity of infinite supply. The more we ask for, the more we get.

I recently had a client who claimed to be hopeless. Her life had spun out of control. She called to say that her burdens were too great to bear. Too many tragedies, too much loss, total despair. "By this time tomorrow," she claimed, "you won't have to worry about me bothering you with my calls. Suicide is the only way out." I prayed for a few seconds before responding. "That's fine," I said, "but do me a final favor. Call someone else before you do yourself in. Anyone. Just pick up the phone book and point to a name." "Why?" she asked. "Because," I said, "when they check your records, I don't want to be known as the grief counselor who took your final call. It'd be awfully bad for my business." With that, she howled. Humor did what solemnity couldn't. Something was released. We're still talking and she's still healing.

As a grief counselor my work is essentially the same as a preacher's. I'm charged with drawing people into faith. My demeanor, my attitude, my understanding, my unconditional love, my life must lead to spiritual connections. It is through such connections that spirits are renewed and that death, as demonstrated by our Lord, is overcome. In this godless society in which we live, those of us who believe must make as many connections as humanly—and divinely—possible. We must tell our stories and help others to tell theirs. We must become walking epistles.

CRY OUT TO HIM IN PAIN

REVEREND DR. CALVIN BUTTS

When I was a teenager, I made a mistake. I participated in a prank that turned sour. Accusations were leveled against me, and the accuser visited my home. Though the prank was minor—we had hidden a

radio from one of our classmates—my parents were understandably upset. That made me upset. The last thing I wanted to do was to bring aggravation upon my mother and father. I felt deeply ashamed and, not knowing what to do, I turned to prayer. As I solicited God's forgiveness, I fell to the floor. I cried. I shook. I perspired profusely. I stayed on my knees for an hour. I didn't move until my body unaccountably began to cool off. My tears dried up. And, just like that, I felt light as a feather. My shame lifted. I felt peace. I went to sleep with an assurance that I had been forgiven. From that moment on, I have never questioned the spirit of God and its ability to heal, deliver, and free me of my burdens.

Decades later I had a similar experience on my birthday. Something was off about the day; something was off about my emotional stability. So I fell on my knees in my study and prayed until peace came—peace without explanation, peace without analysis, peace without conditions. Simple, loving, calming, reassuring peace.

Jesus is the God of peace. He loves, He calms, He reassures. He transforms our anxieties into security. And if you can't experience this for yourself, you can experience the phenomenon by hearing another—teacher, preacher, stranger, or friend—tell the story of his or her transformation. Beyond words, the phenomenon can be expressed in other forms. Music is a fine example. I once asked the great jazz saxophonist Sonny Fortune to play for us at our Abyssinian Baptist Church in Harlem. His heartfelt performance was nothing short of miraculous. He himself was transformed by the eloquent beauty of his music and its healing proper-ties. The congregation was transformed. People were saying, "That's it. That's the spirit, that's the truth, that's the power."

The Holy Spirit leads us to truth and power. That spirit can make you roll in the dust and foam at the mouth. It is not to be taken lightly. It is to be respected. Its purpose is to use us. We must allow that use. We must be open to its energy. Surrender to its force. Trust its intent. Follow its lead.

The Holy Spirit leads us to the one truth that will set us free: that God loves us, whoever we are. That God accepts us, whatever we did. That God embraces us, wherever we may be. That God not only loves us, but that He loves extravagantly and unconditionally.

At the same time, unconditional love carries an obligation. I am responsible to love everyone the way God loves. I am my brother's keeper. I must recognize that my need for material and spiritual comfort means nothing without recognizing the same need in others. My ministry means nothing if it doesn't have concrete purpose in the realm of practical politics. My sisters and brothers must have food, shelter, and safety. My sisters and brothers must be safe from crime. They must be able to pay their rent. They must have justice. In other words, if God loves me, my way of thanking God is by loving someone else. By loving you, my prayer is that you may come to know the God that loves me. But in the meantime, that love must be realized in the down-to-earth terms of the real world.

When hope has been dashed, when there is no place to turn, when shame and guilt have clouded your horizons, you must be taught to turn to God. You cry out to Him in pain. You speak to Him in the language of your heart. You come to Him as you are. You give Him the burdens that weigh you down during the day and the fears that keep you up at night. You confess your sins.

My belief is that we're only saved in spots. I know I'm still a sinner. A big one. But I'm reassured that God knows what I'm going through. I'm reassured that He accepts me as I am. I know I'm cool with God. I know that because every day in every way He is the catalyst, the motivator, the moving force that keeps my life expanding in positive directions. When I surrender myself to Him, my life becomes His and His becomes mine. And there is nothing more beautiful, peaceful, or righteous.

THE MYSTERY OF HISTORY

REVEREND ELLIOTT GREENE

Mysteries
attract us. In
literature and
in life, they
intrigue us.
They call to us
because, once
revealed, they
promise truth.
And what can
be more
exciting,
enlightening,
and liberating
than the
revelation of
truth?

The greatest mystery—the mystery of all history—is revealed, simply and eternally, through Christ.

A cornerstone is a mystery as well as a miracle. We don't understand why its perfect properties—its exact proportions and positioning—are essential in creating a foundation of absolute integrity. Christ is the agent of creation; Christ is the cornerstone. Without a cornerstone, the edifice housing our lives, our spirit, and our faith cannot stand.

In Ephesians 2:20 we read that the apostles and prophets are built upon that cornerstone, "in whom all the building, being fitted together, is growing into a holy temple in the Lord." With a cornerstone in place, we too are able to grow, our foundation strengthened, our holiness deepened.

The cornerstone is most critical to the foundation because it determines the appearance, placement, and function of every other building block. The prophets and apostles become those blocks; they complete the foundation; they fit solidly in place. Through their testimonies, they witness to the veracity of the agent of their creation, Jesus. In much the same way, we too are part of the grand structure. The magnificent architecture of our spirituality hinges on the cornerstone of Christ.

The mystery of our own personal history is resolved in acknowledgment of Christ as both author and architect of creation. Our salvation and freedom as new creations in Christ are based upon the building block of His redemptive powers.

Our bodies may be only a few cents' worth of assorted chemicals, but God has graciously given us greater worth. He has given us vision to see who He is—and who we can be through Him. Through his living Word, God enables us to discern the miracle of the cornerstone. Believe in the cornerstone and know that nothing can destroy the foundation.

The church in which I grew up didn't have a lot of labels. The quintessence of the church's belief can be stated in three words: *God is sovereign.* God is king. God is using his kingship to shed grace upon us. That was the cornerstone of my grandmother's theology. Through good fortune, I've been blessed to attend educational institutions my grandmother never knew existed. I've been blessed to both study and teach mathematics; literature, theology, Hebrew, and Greek. I've had the privilege of examining the nuances of Judeo-Christian thought; of reading the great rabbis, ministers, monks, and priests; of examining the beauty of their meditations and the acuity of their minds. Yet for all the complexities that stimulate my imagination, I go back to my grandmother's simple wisdom.

Her heart knew the truth—that Christ is the one who fulfills our salvation; He is the Lord who saved me; He is the Son of God. As assistant pastor and theologian-in-residence at the New Saint Peter's Presbyterian Church in Dallas, Texas, I teach that the crowning touch of Jesus' ministry is His willingness to submit to the Lordship and Fatherhood of God. We are asked to do the same. This is our crowning touch as well. Our salvation is our submission, for we can do nothing for God except to faithfully yield to His power, plan, and love in Christ.

Jesus, His Father, and His Spirit are one, the startling answer to the mystery of history, the mystical cornerstone upon which unalterable truth is built with perfect and precious precision.

HE'S NO FARTHER THAN A THOUGHT AWAY

CANDI STATON

When we were
still kids, my
sister and I
joined the
Jewel Gospel
Trio. Traveled
everywhere.
Did shows
with Mahalia
Jackson, Paul
Robeson, and
Reverend C. L.
Franklin and
his young
daughter
Aretha. For a

little girl from a little village in Alabama, it was thrilling. Took a long time to learn we weren't being treated fairly. By then I was seventeen and ready to leave. I turned down a scholarship to Tennessee State, got married, and started having kids.

My marriage was miserable. I was seriously frightened. Completely trapped. I still went to church. Fact is, I never left the church. Truth is, I hated the church. I'd seen so-called church people cheat me when I was a child. Now, as a young adult, I saw even more hypocrisy. I saw preachers, bishops, elders—I saw them all lying for money. I saw singers swigging down whisky before running down aisles praising God. I saw my father-in-law, a minister himself, preaching the harsh gospel of condemnation. I saw so much that my heart was sick, my soul in despair, my body weak from beatings.

When I finally saw a way out—singing rhythm and blues—I grabbed it. Left my husband, placed my kids in different homes, and started down the secular road. The road wasn't easy—especially at first—but eventually it was paved with gold. I married a famous soul singer who turned out to be a womanizer, but by then I was my own woman. Or so I thought. My first big hit was "I'd Rather Be an Old Man's Sweetheart (Than a Young Man's Fool)." By now it's the wild days of the free-flying sixties, and I'm flying as high as anyone. I reject the church. I reject God. To my little way of thinking, God hadn't been good to me while the world was showering me with favor. Big cars, big diamonds, big furs. I'm drugging and drinking and living in the clubs. I'm convinced that everything's more real in the clubs than in the churches. The devil's in the clubs for sure; the devil's sure enough in me; but at least the devil ain't pretending to be something he ain't. I divorce the star. And keep making hit records.

I go through more men. One is a pimp. He's pimping women, and he's pimping my voice. Another is a coke addict who gets saved. When he tries to get me back in church, I say no. "You go on, brother. Knock yourself out." I'm still resenting God until God saves my life. I'm in a brutal car accident that should have killed me. Being physically saved, I realize I need to be spiritually saved. All I can think of is Jesus. He enters my heart. I enter His. Everything changes. I cancel my tour. I dedicate my life to Him.

Now it's 1982. How am I going to make a living? Doing what I did when I was a kid—singing gospel.

But I discover the gospel world is cold. Cliquish. I'm not accepted in that world. Can't make a living. Have to put my kids in the welfare lunch program. The struggle deepens. Black Christian stations say I sing too white; white Christian stations say I sing too black. At my lowest ebb, I'm on the floor, on my knees, asking God, "How much more can I take?" That's when I hear angels singing, "When He speaks to my heart, I can hear Him say, 'I'm not farther than a thought away.'" The same week I write the song, "He's No Farther Than a Thought Away." Praise the Lord television network opens its door to me. Jim Bakker becomes my biggest fan. Later, at Trinity Broadcasting, Jan and Paul Crouch become even bigger boosters. Takes a long time, but black churches start to accept me. And in the meantime, God gives me dozens of songs. I can't stop writing, can't stop singing, can't stop praising Jesus.

So I've returned to the place where I started as a little girl. Only this time I've been to hell and back. I know what I'm singing about. I know life without God. And I know life with God. I know my mission is to introduce audiences to a loving savior. I'm not talking religion. I'm talking relationship. I'm not talking condemnation. I'm talking grace. My sins are paid for. Forgiven. Forgotten. My life is renewed, better than ever. When I come up short—and you know I will—God won't kick me to the curb. He'll embrace me. He'll say, "Candi, you are my child. You are loved."

TURN, TURN, TURN

PASTOR REGINALD T. JOHNSON, JR.

At thirty-five, I'm blessed to lead a young congregation in an old church, Cornerstone Baptist of Baltimore, Maryland. Our church was founded by wise men who gave a good word. I've tried to adapt and

relax the church to welcome everyone. I say, come as you are. Whatever your dress, whatever your lifestyle, Jesus will meet you where you are.

I don't teach religion. I teach relationship. You can have religion without having a relationship with Christ. Folks do a lot of things religiously. You can religiously attend church. Religiously go to the hairdresser. Religiously play the lottery. But acting religiously can isolate you. Some feel because they're part of a particular religion, they can't be around certain people. This guy doesn't smell right. This gal doesn't look right. But that's not Jesus' ministry; that's not the ministry we're instructed to model. The Lord didn't hang out with the good people. He went to the sinners. He came to seek and save those who are lost. He said, Here I am. Know Me. Love Me. Relate to Me.

I am not a compromising preacher. I preach the Word as it is. I give it to you straight. But I always stress that while the Word of God cuts, it also heals. Yes, it cuts to heal. Penetrates to cleanse; shocks you to save you; enters you to illuminate you; breaks down your resistance to build up your belief. If the Word doesn't move you to action, something's wrong. The whole point of the Word is to change you. Set you on a new direction. Turn you around.

Turn, turn, turn.

I don't believe in using the Word to beat up and batter. I use the Word to awaken, activate, motivate. Let's say you've been running from Jesus. Let's say that, like Jonah, you're avoiding God's plan for you. Jonah ran, but couldn't hide. Ran into a storm. The storm threw him into a wild sea. God will allow some storms to come your way. God will put you in some tight spots. He'll work it so you'll have nowhere to turn but to Him. It's all about turning.

Turn, turn, turn.

In our church, some of our most devout members come out of our drug outreach ministry. They know who they were. And they know where they are. They know it was only the grace of God that turned them around.

Turn, turn, turn.

They know that He gives us what we don't deserve. But He looks beyond what we were, looks beyond who we are, and gives us another chance. It's more than a second chance. The truth is, all of us used that second chance a long time ago. No, sir. It's chance after chance after chance. Think of Paul. Tormented by Satan. Thorn in his flesh. Seeks the Lord three times to remove it. Take this thing away, Lord! Can't live with this thing, Lord! And each time the Lord responds by saying that His grace is sufficient, His strength is made perfect by Paul's weakness. God may not remove our suffering. May not remove our pain. But God gives us the strength to endure. To go through it. To overcome it. In doing so, He draws us closer to Him. That's His comfort.

I take comfort in Psalm 34, which says, "The Lord is near to the brokenhearted and saves those who are crushed in spirit. Many are the afflictions of the righteous, but the Lord delivers him out of them all." That's the message I try to convey. People come every

Sunday with their hurts, bruises, and wounds. Their pain is real. Their pain may be excruciating. But the good news of Jesus Christ is that he takes on those hurts, bruises, and wounds. He absorbs every affliction and humiliation of this world. He absorbs our sins. He transforms our lives by redeeming our lives. We relate to Him. He relates to us. We merge. We transform. Through Christ, we find new energy, new purpose. Through Christ, we realize the best and most beautiful parts of ourselves. Through Christ, we are recovered and delivered. Through Christ, we find strength, confidence, and joy in the very act of magnifying His holy name.

THE
BEAUTIFUL
BUSINESS OF
DOING GOD'S
WILL

CHRIS BURGE

The tug on my heart was undeniable, incredible, irresistible. I had graduated from Brown and was climbing the ladder of high finance at Salomon Smith Barney. I liked my work. I enjoyed the monetary

rewards. But every particle of my moral fiber was pulling me in another direction. Yet how could I leave New York City? How could I give up my fast-track career? How could I attend Bible school in what seemed to me the middle of nowhere—Oklahoma? The real question, though, was—how could I not?

Three years later I returned to New York on fire for the Lord. That fire burns more intensely with each passing day. My passion is for teaching. Several nights a week my Bible studies focus on the applicability of the Word to everyday challenges. My mission is clear: to help people reach their divine potential using biblical principles for personal development. The excitement of the Bible is its absolute relevance to how we live our lives today. I see two kinds of faith. The first, as found in Ephesians 2:8, tells us that by grace we have been saved through faith. Then there's also the faith that shows us how to appropriate and manifest the benefit of being Christian. That faith is rooted in a deep understanding of the Word. We do the Word a tremendous disservice when we fail to honor it with close and careful study. We long to hear the heartbeat of Jesus. By ingesting the Word, though, we *feel* that heartbeat in every passage. The Word *is* the heartbeat of our Lord.

The Word explains our equity of character. We yearn for righteousness—to be in right standing, to be in good position with God. To be right with God means scoring 100 on the test. But no one but Jesus could score 100. Then came the cross. Because of the completed work of the cross, Jesus lets you sign your name next to His. That's what it means to be "in Christ." The same relationship

Christ has with His Father is now available to you. You have equity—equity of who you are at your core. At your core you're born again. "If anyone is in Christ," says 2 Corinthians 5:17, "he is a new creature." This new equity of character, this new spiritual currency, transforms every aspect of your life. Peter says this new you is born of incorruptible seed. That seed is the very nature of Christ dwelling within.

The new you—the new me—is fed by new insights into the Word. My Bible study, for example, has spent six weeks on the little four-chapter book of Ruth and gleaned a lifetime of learning. The more you delve, the more the Holy Spirit reveals. The goal is always to make the most of this season of your life. The goal is always to discern between the convicting nature of the Holy Spirit, which is specific, and the generalized condemnation of Satan. Satan will cover you with self-loathing. He is a fanatical enemy. In dealing with his fanaticism, you can't be a casual saint. You must be attentive and assertive. You must understand that Satan's attack is an endorsement of your potential. But somehow he'll blind you to that potential. Satan uses shame to imprison you. Satan knows you can't accomplish what God desires when low-grade guilt beats you down. Satan doesn't want you to think you're forgiven. He wants to keep you in turmoil, remorse, and eternal regret. But a righteous reading of the Word will erase that misunderstanding. A righteous reading will set you free in God's glory and grace. A righteous reading will restore your equity of character.

You don't read the Word for knowledge. "Knowledge puffs

up," says 1 Corinthians 8:1, "but love builds up." You read it for love. You read it—you live it—to access Christ's love. That love allows you to forgive and be forgiven, to break the paralysis of guilt and the bondage of living outside God's value system. That love allows you to incarnate the Word and become, like Jesus, a spirit focused not on self-seeking or willfulness, but rather the beautiful business of doing God's will.

MY JOB IS TO PROCLAIM HIM

REVEREND
DR. OTIS MOSS, JR.

Emerging from the baptismal pool, I caught a glimpse of the eyes of those praying for me—elderly men and women with tears streaming down their cheeks. "I baptized your mother in this very pool," said the preacher,

"and now that she is home with the Lord, I believe that on this day I am baptizing another preacher." In this fleeting moment, I felt the marriage of heaven and earth.

A few years later, I fulfilled his prophecy. My mother died when I was four, my father when I was sixteen. By seventeen, I was preaching the gospel. Rural Georgia didn't exactly encourage education for black men, but, despite difficult economic circumstances, I never doubted that I'd complete both college and graduate school. During seminary, I made a conscious decision to join Martin Luther King, Jr., in the civil rights movement, where I committed my life, as a follower of Jesus Christ, to nonviolence. In 1960, I was leader of a student group about to sit in at the state capitol in Atlanta. We were told—accurately, it turns out—that the

Klan was waiting for us. The night before our demonstration, we were arrested. It was the first time I spent the night in prayer. The next day my heart was free of fear. I believed in the pure righteousness of our mission. The greater mission, of course, succeeded. Yet even if I had died that day, I would have been all right. I was in His will, not mine.

When I was twenty-nine, my wife of five years died of cardiac arrest. As a young man, young father, and young pastor, I struggled with my faith. I spent five days at a retreat, praying, meditating, seeking God. God touched me with blessed assurance. I knew then the presence of Jesus Christ would be the sustaining and guiding principle of my life. Grief galvanized me. That experience of unspeakable pain led to the wisdom that said, "You don't need to ask why. Move on to the next assignment. Minister to others." God blessed me with another remarkable woman who has now been my wife for thirty-eight years. But it took that initial loss to forge my understanding of God as the healer. As a young widower, I further understood that it was my job to proclaim Him. Articulate His Word through my human instrument. Persuade others of His glory.

In our own limited way, we are called to utilize all our God-given energies and powers of reason to demonstrate His love. That means we must be forgiving in our dealings with others, forgiving in our own journeys, forgiving of ourselves. We must be present-tense living examples of what He taught. We are wise to ask the questions—how will love expand our own lives? How will love, although practiced imperfectly, enrich our community? In my teaching, I am constantly referencing the early stage of our civil rights movement. In the ten years I worked with Dr. King, I saw love transform a significant segment of American society. While it's true that many abandoned nonviolence as an instrument of change, nonviolence is not defeated. Just as the risen Christ could not be defeated by death, neither can love be defeated.

We struggle to know His will. Often that's not easy. That's why submitting to the struggle is critical. Like so many truths, the notion is couched in paradox: We arrive at clarity by confessing our confusion. To my congregation in Cleveland, the Olivet Institutional Baptist Church, I like to preach on the paradox couched in Psalm 139. The psalmist talks about God's intimate knowledge of us, His omnipresence and the miraculous way in which He made us. The psalm is a powerful testimony to prayer. But the positive prayer is unexpectedly interrupted: "Do I not hate those who hate you, O Lord? And do not I loathe those who rise up against You? I hate them with the utmost hatred; they have become my enemies." Those verses are often left out. But I read them as an honest expression and struggle of the psalmist's heart. He closes by saying, "Search me, O God, and know my heart; try me and know my anxious thoughts; see if there be any hurtful way in me, and lead me in the everlasting way." The psalmist questions his previous negativity. He knows enlightenment depends upon the reconciliation of his mind with the mind of God. This is the struggle—the noble struggle—to do God's will.

JESUS MEETS US WHEREVER WE ARE

PASTOR
WILLETTE A. BURGIE

Discipleship is a journey—a journey with Jesus, to Jesus. As Director of Student Formation and Seminary Chaplain at Eastern Baptist Theological Seminary in Philadelphia, my job is to facilitate that journey for

those preparing for Christian ministry. Here we strive for a community and worship life that is diverse, exciting, and meaningful. Our aims are to nourish and challenge. One of the ways we achieve those objectives is through discipline born out of love.

I think of Bartimaeus in Mark 10:46, the blind man who sat by the side of the road. As he heard the Messiah approaching, he cried out, "Jesus, son of David, have mercy on me!" Jesus heard him and healed him. It strengthens our patience and practice as disciples to consider: How long had Bartimaeus been waiting there? How did he sharpen the senses of his hearing and his heart so that he would recognize when the Savior was present?

Christian spiritual disciplines—prayer, worship, fasting, silence, meditation on Scripture, service, anonymous generosity, journaling, and others—are all ways of sitting by the side of the road in anticipation of Jesus' approach. Discipline is a form of patience, focused training in small parts that enable the whole to appear almost effortless when all the elements come together. Just as great athletes use disciplined practice to gain a relaxed freedom in the execution of their game, our Christian spiritual disciplines gain us freedom in our faithful walk of discipleship.

Christian discipleship is purposed to work a transformational miracle—we are being transformed into the image of God's own Son. We look to Jesus, the "author and finisher of our faith." He disciplined Himself to do His Father's will, and our discipline is to follow Him. When we do, we must marvel at how He received people, how warmly He embraced them, how deeply He accepted and loved them. One of the great mysteries of ministry for me is—How did He do that? He saw sin, He saw human frailty, He saw disease, He saw injustice, He saw cruelty, dishonesty, and betrayal. He saw it all. But somehow He maintained a focus that enabled Him to shine as a beacon of love. That's why folks flocked to Him. That's how His ministry spread. That's why we are drawn to Him, not only as our Savior, but also as our confidant and our inspiration to live a compassionate, focused life of discipleship.

To be formed into the image of Christ is to be transformed. The process of transformation is the work of the Holy Spirit, and we cooperate with Him through our spiritual diligence, which is not always easy. When fasting, you may get dizzy, you may get headaches; but at the right time, the fruit of your fasting will prove "the sufferings of this present time are not worthy to be compared with the glory that is to be revealed in us" (Romans 8:18). Like blind Bartimaeus, your diligence brings you where God wants to meet you, and there you will get from God what only God can offer.

In the small congregation that meets in my home, there is something I've said so often that everyone has it memorized: "Just *be* where you are." Too often we think—and I've been guilty of this myself at times—that God requires purity of us before we can approach Him. If we harbor malevolent impulses, we feel unworthy of His company. So what do we do? We pretend that we're "holier than thou," that we're mature in the spirit and have mastered the sinful impulses that torment us. We perpetrate pseudo-perfect identities. When we do that, though, we miss Him. He's looking for the real me, the real you. He knows—and was cruci-fied for—your true and flawed identity. If you drink in His Word, you'll understand that He wants you, like Him, to be authentic. Authenticity means honesty, honesty from the surface to the depths. Honesty means being yourself, and admitting where you are on the journey. And no matter where you are on the journey, He can find you there. He does not leave us the same way He finds us—once He finds us, He shapes us and corrects us and heals us and uses us through both comfort and suffering. With Jesus, com-fort and suffering constitute the ebb and flow of our lives. But if we stay authentic on our journey of Christian discipleship, we don't have to worry about arriving at our destination: Jesus' love meets us where we are, and stays with us all the way Home.

HE IS THE SONG

PASTOR MARVIN L. WINANS

I got saved on February 12, 1970, in a little storefront church in Hamtramck, Michigan, during a fifteen-day revival led by Mother Estelle Boyd. I was eleven. The spirit of the Lord said to me, "If I save

you, would you be willing to give up your friends?" I said, "Yes, Lord." Then the Holy Ghost just filled me up. And I was given songs.

I never had piano lessons. Never had formal training. The training was all in the spirit. My first song came down like gentle rain. "God is a miracle worker," I began to sing. "God is a glorious God." By the time I was thirteen, I had written a hundred songs. They just flowed. And then one day I'm walking down the street, just singing and talking to God, when the Lord says, "These songs are not just for you." Another epiphany, another realization that my songs—like God's gifts—are designed to be shared. Next time I look up I've written five hundred songs. Folks ask, "How can you write so many?" I answer, "I don't write them, I live them. I don't try to birth them, I just breathe them." Sometimes the Lord wakes me in the middle of the night and gives me the most wonderful melody. Thank you, Jesus. Sometimes I lose the melody and pray for its return. When it doesn't return, I understand that the melody came only to console me. When it does return, I realize it's for everyone. Either way, I praise God for the ability to vent. Nothing stays bottled up in me. Jesus allows me to sing what others feel.

As a young boy, growing up in an amazing musical family, I was never tempted by the secular side. Michael Jackson and I are the same age, and I was crazy for the singing of the Jackson Five. Michael's voice thrilled me. But I realized that my calling was to magnify the Lord. I believed then—as I believe now—that gospel is the greatest of all music. Gospel isn't tied to the material world.

Gospel can take you to the heights of divine revelation. Gospel goes deeper and gospel goes higher. Gospel soars.

As a young man, I went to Los Angeles and had all sorts of offers to sing all sorts of music. But no, thank you. Once the Lord got a hold of me as a little boy, His hold held. All I wanted was Him.

I preached my first sermon on December 18, 1976, when I was eighteen.

Thirteen years later I founded my own congregation, the Perfecting Church in Detroit. The church has grown tremendously, and the church remains with me wherever I travel. I see the church as the heart of God inside my heart.

I also feel God inside me when I sing with my brothers. When we perform in Tokyo, for instance, to a non-English-speaking audience, I see our Japanese fans mouthing every lyric to every song. When we sing a Beatles medley, God breaks into those lyrics as well—instead of "Yesterday," it's "Calvary, that's the place where Jesus died for me"; it's "Something in the way He moves me … something about God's grace"; it's "The long and winding road that leads to heaven's door." God is in every song. He *is* the song.

God's song makes sense of sound. God makes sense. God orders chaos. That's true in a super-broad cosmic way, and also true in a personal way. God asks us to surrender to our significance. We are significant in His sight. And we must give that significance back to Him. Look how He reached the Samaritan woman. In John 4, we see that He knew her past. He speaks to her directly. He puts her in touch with herself. "God is spirit," He tells her, "and those who worship Him must worship in spirit and truth." It's beautiful how Jesus puts all of us in touch with ourselves. Until we know Him, we don't know ourselves. Just as He shapes the universe with awesome unity, He shapes our lives. If we allow Him to mold us, we experience a unity of the soul. We move from chaos to calm serenity; suddenly we make sense; suddenly we reflect a spirit that calms our fears even as it excites our faith. Yes, He is the song. And once we accept Him, He becomes *our* song.

I AM
A SERVANT

BISHOP ALICE POPE

I wanted to care for people. Even as a little girl in a little country town in Texas, I had a nurturing heart. My first choice was to be a doctor, but financially that wasn't possible. As a domestic, my mother worked many jobs to make

ends meet. As the oldest of seven, I had to chip in. I became a nurse. Then, in spite of my reluctance and apprehension, the Lord birthed forth my ministry. I never wanted to create a problem for the church. Didn't believe in women preachers. Didn't want to preach. Didn't understand where the Holy Spirit was leading me, so I resisted. But increasingly I found myself in leadership positions. I wanted people to see Jesus, not me. I saw, however, that meant allowing people to see the Jesus *in* me. That meant opening myself more to Jesus and His Father's will. I was always strong in the Word, and the Word says God loves an obedient spirit.

I helped young men set up new ministries. At one we congregated in the chapel of a mortuary. That required, both before and after services, moving bodies in and out. I didn't complain. I was moving the dead to reach the living. I saw it as God's work. I saw that work manifest itself in my job at the hospital. One day a patient, who was Catholic, asked me to lay hands on her. She knew my background was Baptist but didn't care. She had uterine cancer. James 5:15 and 16 speaks of healing the sick, and I believe the Word. I asked her if she believed God would heal her. She said yes. I lay hands on her. She began speaking in tongues, although she knew nothing about tongues. Her next X-ray and ultrasound showed no trace of cancer. Now suddenly women were lining up and down the hallway. I worried about getting fired. My job was to heal medically, not spiritually, but I couldn't refuse. God birthed forth the healing.

God birthed forth my ministry in the parks of South Central

Los Angeles, where I fed the homeless four times a week. People warned me; they said those parks were overrun by gangs. But I couldn't worry about that. My mission was ordained by God. I brought my pots and pans and served the hungry. When I was told the gangs—the Crips and the Bloods—were about to fight, I'd walk in between them and push them apart. Not because I'm bold. Or even brave. I am nothing. It is God who gives confidence and strength. Once when I grabbed a young man on the verge of violence, he threatened me with curses. "I love you," I told him, "but I'll break your neck if you don't shut your mouth." He shut his mouth. "You will end up either dead or in prison," I told the others. "God has more for you than that."

My home became a drop-in not only for believers, but for

those struggling with drugs and drink. One night a big-time dope dealer called my sister and said he was going to kill me for hurting his business in the park. "Tell him I'll be in the park at noon tomorrow feeding the hungry," I said. "If he wants to kill me, it won't be hard." Next day was pouring rain. I spotted a fancy car across the street from my pots and pans. I felt eyes watching me. An inebriated homeless man came to be fed, but started screaming with impatience. Next thing I know, the fancy car pulls closer. The dope dealer emerges. He doesn't look at me. He looks at the poor homeless soul. He tells him to be patient and grateful for what I'm doing. Then I turn to the dealer and say, "God gave me a Word for you. You're called to preach." Right then and there he breaks down and cries like a baby. I hold him in my arms—and never see him again.

My ministry, Agape New Testament, both as a church and a force for social action, has worked miracles—in private houses, in hospitals, in big cities like L.A. and small towns like Hallettsville, Texas. I go to nursing homes. I minister to those in comas, those leading marginal lives. My joy is to go to swap meets and meet people looking to swap their fears for faith. If they ask who I am, I say, "I am a servant." If they ask me what I believe, I say, "I believe in Jesus, deliverer, confidant, raiser of the dead. Believe in Him and accept His gifts. Be healed. Be delivered. Be loved."

ENCOMPASSED IN TRANQUILLITY

REVEREND ALTAGRACIA PEREZ

My dad is Dominican, my mom Puerto Rican. I grew up in the Bronx, with a picture of Our Lady of Altagracia, patron saint of the Dominican Republic, hanging above my bed. A glow-in-the-dark rosary lit

my nights and comforted my little-girl soul. The chaos of my early life was, to some degree, mitigated by the Catholic church. The giant space of the church, dark with candles, bells, and incense, felt holy and safe. I felt encompassed in tranquillity. A little later I was rebaptized in a small Baptist church and, at age fifteen, received my call to ministry. The predominantly Puerto Rican Baptist congregation was charismatic in character and extremely conservative theologically. I immersed myself in its teachings and preached a sermon to a youth group when I was fifteen. Some said that, like Jeremiah, I was to be a prophet; others said that I was called to speak in tongues and interpret God's will for others. I never received those gifts, though my passion for serving the Lord stayed strong. I was skeptical at how some used fear to control the congregants. But no matter, I set off for college determined to enlighten my mind and soul.

In my senior year at New York University a professor of religion and social issues shocked me by plainly stating that he did not consider homosexuality a sin. I literally looked up and waited for a bolt of lightning to strike him dead. But he was not struck down for saying it; nor was I was destroyed for considering it. I spent my next four years at Union Theological Seminary, where I earned a master's in divinity and sacred theology. That educational experience rocked my world and radicalized my love for Christ. I walked in a fundamentalist and walked out a new person. All the tensions that plagued me as a teenager—especially the issue of my bisexuality—were seen in a different light. I was being educated by righteous men and women, sincere scholars and preachers, teachers and theologians, many of whom believed being homosexual or bisexual was not incompatible with being Christian.

Liberation theology as applied to poor people broadened my view of God. While still in seminary, at age twenty-two, I joined the Episcopal church, where I could be myself and not feel estranged from the body of Christ. As an Episcopalian, I was given understanding and acceptance. After graduating, I went to Chicago and did nonprofit work for ten years before being sent to a predominantly and historically black church in South Central L.A. Recently I became the rector at Holy Faith Episcopal Church in Inglewood, California, where I pray with a rich mixture of Africans, African Americans, African Caribbeans, Latinos, and

Anglos. Like many Episcopal congregations, our church has seen conflict. Even though our parish mission statement welcomes all people regardless of race, creed, ethnicity, social position, or sexual orientation, several members were angered—and quit—when I supported Gene Robinson, an openly gay clergyman and loving disciple of Christ, as bishop. When asked about my own sexuality, I identified with the lesbian, gay, bisexual, and transgender community. Some congregants left, but most stayed.

As a happily married woman with four beautiful daughters, I am as devoted to the integrity of the nuclear family as I am to a church that embraces the loving values of Jesus Christ. Jesus chose to be faithful to his mission to redeem us and show us the way, regardless of the cost. That cost was the way of the cross. Our life is a cross as well, and the only way we are reborn is through death—the death of an addiction, the death of idolatry, the death of soul-crippling materialism, the death of any form of prejudice. I believe we suffer many deaths before the big death and experience many resurrections before the big resurrection.

In this world we live a life of meritocracy, which is disastrous. The idea that you work for everything you get and get what you deserve is not God's truth. God's truth gives each of us what we need. God's truth prevents us from falling out of grace. God's truth gives us salvation through eternity. God's truth calls for radical equality and an end to oppression. God's truth, if we live it day by day, if we breathe it like fresh air, encompasses us in tranquillity.

Encompassed in Tranquillity

GOD IS SETTING YOU UP: SITUATIONS FOR REVELATIONS

BISHOP NOEL JONES

My father was a Pentecostal preacher in Jamaica. I grew up in an extraordinarily strict environ-ment and rebelled against what I perceived as narrow scriptural interpretation. Ironically—or purposefully—

when I reached nineteen and heard the call to preach, I realized that my life, like my dad's, would be all about explicating the Word.

I believe in the Word. I believe there is a Word with which God both manifests and reveals His glory. Through the Holy Spirit, we can dissect and illuminate that Word. We can show how that Word gives meaning and hope to the life we live.

Take, for instance, the famous story of Lazarus of Bethany as told in John 11. Jesus loves this little family of a brother and his two sisters—Lazarus, Mary, and Martha. Yet when he hears Lazarus is failing, he waits two days before attending him. He goes so far as to tell his disciples that he is "glad" Lazarus is dead. When Jesus finally arrives in Bethany, Mary and Martha are frantic, crying to the Master, "If you had been here, our brother would not have died."

What's happening here? Where is the Word?

In the canyons of eternity, *logos* is the Word, the awesome force of creative life emanating from the mouth of God. The Word is the reality and totality, the very essence of God. Jesus is a manifestation of the Word. The gospels are a manifestation of Jesus. Gospel stories like Lazarus show God entering history, moving into the circumstances of Jesus' earthly ministry. To reveal His Word, God enters lives and sculpts circumstances. Jesus enters the life—and what seems to be the irreversible death—of Lazarus.

As pastor of the City of Refuge in Gardena, California, I can only speak in normal grammatical terms to my congregants. But it takes God to insert the Word into your heart. I speak to you intellectually; God speaks to you spiritually.

God creates situations for revelation. He inserts himself into your life circumstances, not on your timetable, not according to your expectations or demands, but according to His revelatory plan. Jesus inserted Himself into the life of Mary and Martha, not when they called Him, but when the revelatory moment was ripe.

He had a Word for their brother, dead in his tomb: "Unbind him. Loose him. Let him go." God has a Word for you: "Unbind yourself. Loose yourself. Let yourself go."

God set up the sisters.

Through your trials, your pain, your failures and fears, God is setting *you* up. With a mighty hand, God is getting ready to show *you* what only God can show. Just as he gives fresh life to Lazarus, he gives fresh life to *you*.

Like Martha and Mary, we may think God is late. But like the old folk used to say, "God may not be there when You want him, but He's always right on time." His Word is eternal, wondrous, and true.

Like Lazarus, so many of us are considered hopeless. Dead. But in Jesus there is no death, only victory. And you're getting ready to be victorious. Empowered. Ennobled. Energized.

You might be wrapped up, tied up, and messed up, but there is a Word. You might be down and depressed, imprisoned in despair, but I say there is a Word.

And that Word, glorious and righteous, will release you from every form of bondage. That Word is Jesus.

Jesus is the living Word, the stabilizing force that gives you the internal strength to take on all negative forces.

When you know Him—when knowledge of Jesus is formidable in your system—you have a steadiness of purpose, a clarity of direction, a moral focus, a spiritual bedrock.

When you know Jesus, you don't worship the pastor, deacons, or elders. You don't worship grandiloquence. You worship Him.

When you know Jesus, you find Him working for you, working *in* you, stretching you, motivating you, blessing you beyond your wildest dreams.

You can't outlive Him, and you can't live without Him.

As the good shepherd dies to save his flock, He died to bring you life.

Yet His life defeated death. His life lives in you.

And the very essence of His life—love—lasts forever.

THE IRRESISTIBLE PULL

REVEREND GEORGIA
HILL THOMPSON

After high school, I went off to Harvard, which was something of a shock—the racism I encountered in certain sections of Boston, the extreme affluence of some of my classmates, the reactionary

stance of the school itself. It was the late seventies, when South Africa was much on our minds. I saw the world divided between the haves and have-nots. I marched with the radicals. I became a radical. My politics may have been enlightened, but darkness surrounded me. As the child of a doctor in middle-class Detroit, I was raised Christian but suddenly found myself outside my Christian walk. I wanted acceptance by my peer group of right-thinking radicals. Politically and socially, I wanted to be hip. I did some outlandish things. I excluded God from my life.

When I graduated at twenty, I moved to Washington, D.C., where I worked for an African American newspaper and then a research and development firm. I decided to go to law school at Howard, which was a phenomenal experience because, as part of the Equal Opportunity Litigation Clinic, I was able to argue in front of the U.S. Court of Appeals. In law school, though, the party continued. I was still overcompensating for being a good girl from a good home who spoke the King's English. I was still looking to be accepted on others' terms, not God's. I didn't live with the certain knowledge that God had already accepted me. Slowly, though, something started to shift.

It started with friends in law school who were Christian, women whose simple kindness and consideration reminded me of something I had forgotten: that God acts through people. I began attending church. It helped that the church encouraged casual dress. I loved being able to seek the Lord in comfortable clothes. I started to relax. Later I would understand that the state of relaxation—the ease and comfort of knowing that God is love and that God is real—was critical to my renewal of faith.

I went home to Detroit, where as an attorney I practiced product liability and from there went into corporate work. For over a decade, I practiced law, initially with the biggest law firm in Michigan. It was there that I started feeling a pull, like a rope tied to my waist. At first the pull was subtle, then significant, then strong, then stronger, and finally irresistible. I call it the irresistible pull of God. The call of God. The heart of God drawing me, illuminating me, exciting me. The view from my office high over the Detroit River looked on Canada; but I kept seeing Chicago. I kept hearing "seminary . . . seminary in Chicago." So I went to Chicago and visited the McCormick Theological Seminary, where, during a student-led service, I felt the breath of the Holy Spirit upon my heart. After graduation I was ordained as a minister.

My ministry at Plymouth United Church of Christ in Detroit is about breaking down the Word of God to make it understandable. Applicable. Alive in our lives. I love decoding and demystifying the Bible. I love conveying its message that God is calling us to do mighty exploits. I'm convinced that as we devote our lives to Christ our lives become larger. Our role as leaders becomes essential. The church should not be following corporate America. The church ought to be leading corporate America. I'm not comfortable when the church adopts corporate models without applying biblical wisdom. In some churches the pastor is now called the CEO. It's the CEO, in fact, who should be learning from the church.

Church leaders should be developing innovations for management based on biblical, not worldly, principles.

The point of our mighty exploits, the point of enlarging our lives must be directed to Christ. Our job is to magnify His Glory. It is His Glory that frees us to express all that is good—all that is God—within us. As a pastor, if I take the glory, I miss the point. If I fail to lead you to Christ, I miss the mark. My job is to get you to fall in love with Jesus. I try to do that by living the life—the new life, the transformed life, the relaxed, the beautifully spiritual life—which He has, through His grace, granted me. Everything that has happened to me, from Harvard to Howard, from Detroit to Boston to Chicago, has led me back to this single idea: I can't just talk about what the Bible says; I have to live it.

SACRED FOUNTAIN OF CREATIVE BEAUTY

KIRK WHALUM

I call it the Encounter. I was fourteen and at Baptist camp. I wasn't looking for God; I was looking for girls. My hormones were raging. I'd gotten drunk for the first time in my life. I was crazy with teenage

energy. Then a pastor with a heart for young people prevailed upon us to pray. And in one such prayer—don't ask me how, don't ask me why—I felt the reality of God. I felt the personal reality of Jesus. I felt Him touching my heart, entering my heart, changing my heart. I had feelings of tremendous culpability and guilt followed by feelings of tremendous relief. I couldn't stop crying. For the first time, I knew the Lord.

The second Encounter happened when I was twenty and a student at Texas Southern University. My English class assignment was to analyze a biblical passage. No problem. My dad's a preacher. I thought I knew the Bible. But when I opened to the page containing the passage, I was faced with a dead roach. The roach startled me. It stared at me. Time stood still. It had been six years since

Christ had come into my life. That had been a beautiful thing. But the truth is that I never sat down and actually read the Bible. I saw the dead roach as a symbol of my ignorance. The book was alive, but I was not alive to the book. Now I had to read it. And I did. And I'm still reading it. And will always be reading it. What I learned is that God lives in this book as He lives in us—a force of eternal energy, a source of brilliant enlightenment.

Thank God my parents' enlightenment allowed me to pursue my craft as a jazz musician without shame or remorse. I was made to understand that it was not a contradiction to play jazz and serve God. The older I became, the more I understood that the source of jazz, like the source of all creativity, *was* God. Because our tradition so closely links music to faith, I see my faith in jazz linked to my faith in God. Our music was born from the fertile ground of faith—the field shouts, the spirituals, the blues, the rhythm and the blues, the songs of praise. The many genres are really one genre: the music-as-faith genre—faith in the fact that the outpouring of honest emotions is a basic form of prayer; faith in the power of art as an expression of Love Supreme; faith in the notion that when we experience music we experience the essential mystery and beauty of God's soaring spirit.

My spirit is in jazz. I am a proud practitioner of the art form. On my finger I wear a ring worn by the great Texas tenor-man Arnett Cobb. I respect my jazz elders as parishioners respect church elders; they are my spiritual mentors. And the more I play, the more I preach, both on my horn and through words spoken on the bandstand. At a recent concert I started talking about my feelings for the Lord. Afterward one of my musicians was miffed. "When you speak," he said, "people automatically assume you're speaking for us too." I apologized. But at the same time I said, "This is what I have to do. I will understand if you tell me you're not comfortable playing behind me anymore. But my testimony is my testimony. When I'm moved to witness, I witness."

Jazz itself moves me to witness. For some years I've pursued a precious project called "The Gospel According to Jazz." Under that banner there have been concerts, CDs, and DVDs. I realize that some people encountering the marriage of Jesus and jazz might take offense. But there are times, I believe, when we're supposed to offend. The cross is offensive.

The cross is also our salvation. Jazz lives in the real world. So did Jesus. So *does* Jesus. So if my heart is in jazz, and if my heart is in Jesus, and if I see the two as one, I have to express it through my horn, I have to talk about it. I have to tell the good news.

Jazz is a sacred fountain of creative beauty. So is Jesus. The fountain lives inside us. So does Jesus.

TURN OUR EYES INTO EARS

REVEREND ANTHONY TRUFANT

Moments of disorientation and disjunction can be frightening. They can also be the most critical moments of our lives. During such moments we're receptive as never before. Those moments are life's way of puncturing the illusion of self-

sufficiency. Trauma leads to transition. Breakdowns lead to break-throughs. Confusion leads to questioning. Who am I? Where am I headed? Who's really in charge? When we learn that it's not about position, power, or prestige, when we realize life is really a gift, we move into gratitude. We see that the gift comes in the form of relationships. As human beings, we must relate to one another. As spiritual beings, we must relate to God.

Christ is the prism, the lens through which I look at life. Christ affords us a glimpse into the mind and heart of God. Christ is the highest and clearest revelation of God. When we study Him, when we worship Him, we're given a key to the meaning of existence. The life of Christ is paradigmatic. We follow His footsteps. We emulate His behavior. The more people see us, the less they see us, the more they see Him. As we allow the Holy Spirit to mold us into His nature, our own nature transforms from self-centric to Christ-centric. The transformation is beautiful. Burdens are lifted, anxieties eased, fears assuaged.

I try to equip my members at Emmanuel Baptist Church in Brooklyn with the ability to think biblically and theologically. In the midst of any moment, good or bad, the challenge is to listen long enough to hear what God is saying. That requires turning our eyes into ears. We have to hear what He's saying. We have to feel His prompts. We have to trust those prompts. We have to trust Him. As we grow into the people God wants us to be, we get to experience and manifest Christian maturity. We're calm in the midst of life's turbulence. We're focused on faith.

God's incarnation in Christ reminds us that eternity has entered into time. Our time, the various moments of our days and lives—good and bad, happy and sad—are not discontinuous but building blocks to a fuller understanding of our higher purpose. Because we're human, that purpose will, to some degree, be shaped by ego. Kierkegaard made a distinction between what he called "shaven passion" and "unshaven passion." Unshaven is raw ambition. Shaven, consecrated by God, directs our desires and dreams to pass through the filter of faith. David, for example, dreamed of building a great temple. But God shaved that passion; He modified David's dream, allowing him to prepare the resources and design a blueprint for his son Solomon to build upon. While God may say no to one of our dreams, He continues to use us for a higher plan. We may not know His plan. We don't have to know His plan. We simply have to accept His sovereignty.

God is not only about our personal plan. There's a rich and rewarding dimension to communal worship. Recognizing that we live in the midst of a world that has resisted God's overtures, we bear responsibility for making sure that His love manifests in a public forum. We gather in community to ensure that the peace of God is experienced in a real and tangible expression. We do that by building decent housing, by making sure people have jobs with living wages, by ensuring access to quality health care and quality education. We do that by fighting for social justice. These are the things that illuminate the love of God. We meet people's needs in the name of the God who revealed Himself in Christ.

We look for revelatory moments, teachable moments. We remain in His grace. Aquinas said that grace doesn't eliminate nature, it perfects it. We seek perfection knowing that, falling short, God grants us his perfect love. We seek to comprehend His Word—to live His Word—but we employ other means to illuminate our message. We employ the sacred arts. We praise Him with dance, drama, and music. We know that when the Word is enacted, sung, or danced, defense mechanisms melt. We preach in kindness and understanding, in conviction and strength. We disdain condemnation. No one who feels condemned feels motivated to change. Love is the motivator. Christ is the motivator. His presence defeats fear. His presence overrides condemnation. His passion becomes ours, creativity without end, the eternal here and now.

THE LOVER OF OUR SOUL, THE HONEY IN THE ROCK

PASTOR JACKIE
McCULLOUGH

I was born into a preaching home. Daddy was an inner-city preacher in Jamaica. Mama preached as well. They were grass-roots preachers, not cathedral preachers. They gave to the community, worked with the poor, and

moved us to Manhattan when I was eleven. As a little girl I was petrified. I was ashamed of my accent. I was painfully shy. I didn't take easily to the foreign culture. When I was sixteen, a female bishop laid hands on me and said, "You're going to be a powerful preacher with a strong voice. You're going to preach all over the world." I didn't understand her words, but I felt them. I felt them so strongly that I ran to my mother and wept in her arms.

The bishop's words have come true. Though I became a nurse and planned to become a doctor, God had other plans for me. And because I learned at an early age to be sensitive to God, I had no choice but to follow those plans. God quieted my rebellion. He used my daughter, who died at birth, to draw me closer to Him. He called me to something great. He calls us all to something great. The question is: Will we answer the call?

Looking at the church today, I feel obligated to ask the tough questions: Are we being placated? Are we being challenged? As spiritual leaders, are we patronizing our parishioners out of fear of losing them? Are we more interested in entertainment than ministry? Are we using our gifts, our charms, and our own narrow agenda to manipulate? Are we packaging God's Word to render it pleasant rather than provocative and profound? The Bible says the Word is sharp, quick, and penetrative. It cuts through thinking; it cuts through deceit. It need not be dressed up in frills and lace. It need not be sugar-coated. Its raw power must be exposed, explained, and absorbed.

When Jesus met people, he forced them to make a choice. He said it clearly: "I am the way. I am the truth. I am the life." His is a message of transformation. We must change. If the gospel for which He died cannot produce that change, then how is Christianity different from modern psychology or New Age philosophies?

Without shame, I preach the gospel of Jesus Christ at the International Gathering of Beth Rapha in Pomona, New York, and, for that matter, all over the world. The gospel of Christ is the power of God unto salvation. In plain terms, that means being rescued. If you're not in danger, you don't require rescue. Many of us don't want to discuss the fact that we're all in danger. It is my conviction that we are in dire danger. We must be saved from danger. And to embrace the Savior is to enter into a relationship not unlike marriage. That's the analogy Christ employed. In a true marriage, my spouse knows the worst thing about me yet will not reject me. In a true marriage, I am accepted for who I am. In a true marriage, love will bind all wounds, heal all hurts. Christ proposes a true marriage to each of us. The final question is simple—will we accept His proposal?

In America, we confuse intimacy with sex. But if we spend time nurturing our relationship to the Lord, we will discover a new intimacy whose passion is born of spiritual, not physical, power. There is no greater passion. When we find it, we find the lover of our soul, the honey in the rock, a source of strength without limits.

Since my own father died, God has become a father in a new

and deeper sense. Grief draws us closer to Him. But superficial lifestyles—superficial worship, quickie shouts, and instant salvation—keep us on the outside looking in. We must take Him on. We must take Him in. We must spend time talking and exploring and bonding. We must stop seeking another thrill, another speaker, another star, another conference. We must sit still and drink in His Word. Jesus learned obedience. So must we. We must create intimacy—glowing spiritual intimacy—through the Christ within us. As we are connected to Christ, so must we connect to one another. We must study His book—the whole book—study the author, the social context, the history, the language, the geography. We must study the soil. For it is in that fertile soil that our souls are replenished, our life given new purpose and meaning.

The Lover of Our Soul, the Honey in the Rock

DELIVERANCE AND RECONCILIATION

PASTOR DONNIE McCLURKIN

Once I thought I had nine lives. But those lives have been extended to many more. With each new life comes a new revelation and ever-greater demonstration of God's mercy. With

each new life I'm learning who God is, who I am, and who I am not.

I am not simply an entertainer. I am not simply a singer. I have learned that I am a messenger whose ministry must deliver the simplest of messages: deliverance and reconciliation.

The power of God will deliver you from anything and everything. His love is so absolutely overwhelming that it transcends words. The power of God can also reconcile you to His heart. He can bring you back into relationship with Him. You may not be able to forgive yourself, but He can. He can show you how you are your own worst enemy—how by being harsh with yourself, you cut off the flow of love and compassion; how by striving for perfectionism, you cut off the gifts of humility.

We're prey to legalism, to convictions that convict us, judge us, scorn us, keep us enslaved to self-degradation. For comfort, I go to Psalm 103. The psalmist brings it home when he says, "Just as a father has compassion on his children, so the Lord has compassion on those who fear Him. For He Himself knows our frame; He is mindful that we are but dust." He knows our frailties more than we do. We see how we are prone to failure. Yet the miracle is that our imperfections are reconciled by His perfect love. His love transcends all, forgives us, allows us our humanity while affording us His divinity. He lives within us. He energizes our days and lights our nights. He sends immediate aid when we mess up. His benevolence is infinite.

Legalism only magnifies our failures; it does not magnify

God. Contrary to what legalism preaches, laws are not the focus. His love is the focus. His sacrifice is the focus. His mercy is the focus. If we focus on His true character, fear will fade. We can be free to live holy in God. We'll understand God's role, not as a punitive parent, but as a giver of life. And life more abundant.

My life is centered on ushering people into the presence of God and then backing away. I want them to see Him. Once that's achieved, I'm off to the next assignment. I don't see myself as a celebrity. I can't bless anyone. I can only give someone what He's given me. If anyone gets credit for blessing, it must be Him.

Like anyone, I'm challenged by the world. I'm challenged by what the industry tells me are the accoutrements to which I'm entitled. The other day I had a first-class airplane ticket to Dallas. I was mistakenly put into the coach section, and the worst aisle at that—the very back in a center seat. So I'm sitting there fuming. *How could they dare give my seat away? How dare they cause my discomfort? This is wrong; this isn't fair.* But then God deals with me by telling me to be quiet. God lets me understand I could use three hours of humility. God lets me know, "Donnie, it's not all about you." So I embrace my areas of weakness. I know my basic flaws. I acknowledge them and let Him work on them.

My own work is changing. Just as I reached what the industry calls the pinnacle of singing success, I felt the relentless calling to pastor and preach. To some it might seem like inopportune timing. But it's God's timing, not mine. Our lives are temporal, seasonal. Now I see myself moving into a new season. I've already planned a farewell party for March 2007 for my musical career. I'll continue to sing, but only in the church in which I preach. I say this with joy. My pastoring has become the beat of my heart, my reason for living. I thank God for the clarity that lets me understand how one could become a slave to one's gift. You can't do things because people demand them. You do things for the purpose and passion of God.

My heart is excited by His demands, not the demands of the world. And in following Him, in illuminating His deliverance and reconciliation, I too am delivered by His grace; I too am reconciled to His glory.

HEALED AND SEALED IN GRACE

KIRK FRANKLIN

In serving God, my goal is to be greater offstage than onstage. As a gospel performer— some say a gospel innovator— that hasn't always been the case. I now believe that God used the bad in my life to bring me

closer to Him. For many years I lived in a fog, intoxicated by sex. Those were the years when I pursued a promiscuous lifestyle. I got caught up in a prison of pornography. Ultimately Jesus released me from that prison. Jesus saved me from a life of degradation and hypocrisy. Today I thank Him for my fresh ministry and my new life.

My old life, like my mother's life before me, began in confusion. When my mother was a little girl, her mom was killed. When my mother became pregnant with me, she was fifteen. The woman who raised my mom raised me. At age two, she adopted me. At age four, she changed my name. She became my mama. When I was ten, she was seventy, so there wasn't much talk about sex. The talk was about Jesus. Mama *loved* Jesus. She'd be busting suds and singing about the Lord. At night I'd hear her talking to the Lord.

Her relationship to Christ was powerful and real. Her teaching was straight up: Jesus died so we could exchange our lives for His. He lives in our heart. He *is* our heart. Mama's heart overflowed with His love.

Mama belonged to an old Zion-type church in Fort Worth, Texas, where they sang European-styled hymns. I didn't connect. But at a church across the tracks called Corinth I did connect. That church had the music. Rhythms. Excitement. Holy Ghost power. At Mama's church, though, the pastor saw my talent and paid for my piano lessons. That was a blessing but also a curse because bullies, jealous of my status, would whip me after church. I remember thinking, "This must be how Jesus felt."

At fifteen I was saved. A friend was killed in a freak gun accident, and his death shook me to the core. I got down on my knees and asked Jesus to forgive my sins and become my Savior. I stopped drinking and smoking weed, but sex—and that includes sex with many women from church—was something I didn't stop. Neither did I stop using pornography, which I had started when I was nine.

Born in 1970, I came of age in the eighties. And just as I was developing as a gospel musician, I was deep into the urban music of the day. Hip-hop and break dancing were fresh. I was spinning, pop-locking, doing it all. At the same time, when I trusted Christ with my heart, Christ gave me songs. One song I wrote, "Every Day with Jesus," led me into the national spotlight. In the early nineties, my career took off. Because I was a street kid, my gospel music reflected the streets. My life got exciting, my records sold millions, but seven years later my career dramatically stalled. And so did my spirit.

God used success to break me. He knew that would hurt me the most. I was caught up in my celebrity status, which was as deep as my addiction to sex. I had to see—I had to be taught—that my identity was not in fame, but in Christ. My old walk had ended. My grace walk had begun.

The fact that Christ lives in me changes everything. Christ doesn't want promiscuity. Christ doesn't want pornography. Christ is about loyalty, not cheating; He is about truth, not lies. Christ transforms our lives, day in and day out. Belief in Christ has shown me that real masculinity is found in humility. It took masculinity to stand as Jesus stood, being persecuted, beaten, and tortured. Knowing you possess power but not using that power for your own benefit is the greatest symbol of power. That's what Christ did. He reserved all His divine resources for the sake of sinful man.

My ministry is married to music. In that music is the message of family. We are Christ's family. And though we may come from broken families, our own family can be healed and sealed in grace by serving our Savior. My family—my beautiful wife and our four children—inspire my devotion and gratitude to God for clearing my mind and cleansing my heart. I love being accountable to them. I love being accountable to God. I love the peace that comes with simple obedience. The infidelity of my crazy past has led me to the faith I now practice. That faith—that submission to God's will—is what makes life beautiful.

BUILDING CHAMPIONS FOR DIVINE DEPLOYMENT

BISHOP KENNETH ULMER

I grew up in East St. Louis, Illinois. It was the kind of place, like Nazareth, where they asked, "Could any good thing come out of East St. Louis?" Well, the good thing was a sense of community that revolved

around church. Both my parents were active in various ministries. I grew up in a season when focus was placed on coming into the assembly of God. The gathering together. I studied with a professor at Oxford who contended that our lives must be ordered around our relationship with God. There is a rhythm to that relationship that is rooted in regular attendance and adherence to scheduled worship. For the Jews that meant the Sabbath. For African Americans that meant Sunday-go-to-meeting. There was a discipline inherent in those patterns that anchored our lives and made sense.

As pastor of Faithful Central Bible Church in Inglewood, California, naturally I encourage churchgoing. Our church has been blessed with such phenomenal growth that we worship at the

Forum, where the Los Angeles Lakers once played. From the pulpit, though, my message has evolved. Our challenge, I now feel, is far deeper than merely showing up at church. Our challenge is to know God. Our challenge is to experience the hunger and thirst for the righteousness of God. Our mission statement is that we are building champions for divine deployment. As Christians, our divine responsibility is to be more than recipients of blessings, but channels of blessings. As Dr. E.V. Hill liked to say, "If God can get a blessing through you, He'll get a blessing to you."

Philosophically, this may fly in the face of the last two decades of the contemporary theology that has stressed the *me* in the relationship between me and God: In other words, there was an overemphasis on what God gives me; what I can get from God; God prospering me; God blessing me materially, tangibly, blessing me according to *my* wants, *my* needs. I believe we have bred a generation that seeks the hand of God beyond the faith of God. The value of being in the faith of God, in the presence and revelation of God, is that the light of God might shine through us. The covenant God made through Abraham was more than, "I'm going to bless you," but rather, "I'm going to bless others through you." We are more than a reservoir of God's blessings; we are a river through which God flows.

I'm afraid that today many play to the narcissistic culture that surrounds us. We live in the tension of being authentic and being attractive. I believe we have leaned toward being attractive at the expense of being authentic. The reality of the gospel is that it is not either/or. It is *both*. Authenticity is born out of the attraction of

God's love. Authenticity is the truth of that love. Truth without love is condemnation. And love without truth is compromise. To bring the two into proper balance, to live authentically, to project an attractiveness whose character is formed by the grace of God's love—that is our sacred assignment.

Romans says that "We are more than conquerors," but I believe that we are also champions, we are overcomers. We are the victors God says we are. And we can claim that victory. We can claim it today. But as I do so, I see that the manifestation of this revelation must be brought back into my world. I must take it into my Jerusalem, into my Judea and my Samaria. I must go forth as a champion of Christ.

Someone asked if the words "champions" and "victors" can

foster egotism. They can and often do. That mistake, though, is mitigated the minute we turn to our true champion and embrace the nature of His championship. Jesus' character was about humility. He championed the poor and the downtrodden. His mission was to serve others. His example was obedience. He made it clear that you can't have a testimony until you have gone through a test. The nature of Christ, that many want to minimize, is essential to receiving His gifts: that He reigns because He suffered, and He suffered because He served. It is in the fellowship of His suffering, it is in the wisdom of surrendering to His example, that we are granted strength to overcome any obstacle. And it is through the power of our testimony and example of our lives that we pass on this God-given strength to others.

PRAISING GOD FOR WHAT HE HAS DONE, WORSHIPPING HIM FOR WHO HE IS

PATRICK HENDERSON

I understood early on that He is a God of miracles. I witnessed a miracle when I was eight. My brother Frankie suffered from chronic asthma. His attacks were so severe we feared for his life. One morning Mama was listening

to Oral Roberts on the radio. "There's a woman out there listening to me who has children," he said. "One of them has terrible asthma. I want that mother and those children to place their hands on their radio and pray right now. I want them to know that God will cure that asthma." And so my brother was cured.

My parents were sharecroppers' kids who knew what it meant to praise the Lord. At our house in Dallas they'd have Holy Ghost time—that's what the saints called it—where they'd worship in a way that excited my little heart. Before I was big enough to reach the piano, I played make-believe piano on Mama's dresser, banging out make-believe notes. One night when everyone was dancing with the spirit, someone said, "Patrick is going to get filled tonight with the Holy Ghost. I can feel it." Well, I felt it too. I asked

God to fill me with His love. Next thing I know I'm crying and speaking in tongues and praising, praising, praising.

Instrumentally, the Church of God in Christ was fixated on the Hammond organ. Many great jazz organists performed there, so if you couldn't play for real, they'd shoo you away. By the time I was ten, I was the state organist for the entire denomination. I wasn't a soloist, but a rhythm player. I locked into the spirit of whoever was preaching or singing. They called me a preacher's player. As a young teenager I worked with evangelist S. E. Mitchell. Later when I went to the national convocations in Memphis, I met Mattie Moss Clark, who became a mentor. She was a genius jubilistic composer and ragtime piano player with lightning energy. When Reverend James Cleveland heard me play, he said,

"Whenever I want the church to dance, I'm putting Patrick on the organ."

I learned how to train a choir and taught myself to write. I loved the Beatles and the Temptations, and when I took the groove from "Cloud Nine" and turned it to gospel, the saints went crazy. I was discovered by Leon Russell, who put me onstage with him. He sat at one grand piano while I sat at another. Later I wrote hit songs with Michael McDonald and was hired by Bishop Charles Blake of the West Angeles Church of God in Christ. I was called the Godfather of Praise and Worship because, with Bishop's undying support, I brought that music into the forefront of the African American church. Later I was blessed to lead the Voices of Joy, an amazing six-hundred-member Lutheran choir of Norwegian youth who sing with the precision and passion of the blackest black gospel you can imagine.

A few years back my faith was severely challenged when I was assaulted by a madman. With a sword, he severed my right hand, slashed my face, broke my jaw, and cut me up like a piece of paper. I survived but fell into posttraumatic despair. I became cynical, convinced that God had abandoned me. One day, when I was particularly down, Mama called and said. "You're angry, aren't you? You're angry at God." Mama was right. I had to confess. "But that's good," she added. "How can that be good?" I wanted to know. "Being angry at God means that you're dealing with God. He can take your anger. He can take anything. He can turn cold to hot and hate to love. Keep talking to Him."

I did and eventually saw that He had kept me alive for a reason. I went back to basics. I remembered to praise God for what He has done—given me life. I remembered to worship Him for who He is—love, pure and simple. I remembered that I was taught the meaning of joy by my family, my friends, the saints who loved the Lord with all their hearts and strove to live a holy life. I remembered Mom and Dad taking us back to the country. When my grandmother saw us coming down the road, she'd get to dancing. She'd get so excited she'd jump up and down with unrestrained joy. That's the joy of knowing God and accepting Jesus. That's the joy that lets us get beyond ourselves and enter an altered state of consciousness, a state of bliss. That's the holy joy that's the true definition of heaven on earth, because "the joy of the Lord is our strength."

DAVID RITZ, coauthor of *Howling at the Moon,* is the only four-time winner of the Ralph J. Gleason Music Books Award for Best Music Book of the Year. He has written biographies of Marvin Gaye and jazz singer Jimmy Scott, and coauthored the autobiographies of Ray Charles, B.B. King, Aretha Franklin, the Neville Brothers, Smokey Robinson, and other entertainers. His novels include *The Man Who Brought the Dodgers Back to Brooklyn.* He lives in Los Angeles, California.

NICOLA GOODE, a member of the Society of Motion Picture Still Photographers, has worked on feature films and documentaries for more than fifteen years. Her photographs have appeared in numerous national publications and in galleries in Los Angeles, Prague, and Havana. She lives in Los Angeles.